Network Marketing Masterclass Journal

PERSONAL INFORMATION

This Journal Belongs to _____

Address _____
_____
_____
_____
_____

Business Name _____

Position _____

Contact No. _____

Date __/__/__

Water 🍶🍶🍶🍶🍶

Affirmations

TODAY I AM GRATEFUL FOR

Mindset Rituals

- Meditation
- Audio
- Read

IDEAS	GOALS

Daily Log

BEST THINGS THAT HAPPENED TODAY

Date ___/___/___

Affirmations

Water 🍼🍼🍼🍼🍼

TODAY I AM GRATEFUL FOR

Mindset Rituals

- Meditation
- Audio
- Read

IDEAS

GOALS

Daily Log

BEST THINGS THAT HAPPENED TODAY

Date __/__/__

Affirmations

Water 🍶🍶🍶🍶🍶

TODAY I AM GRATEFUL FOR

Mindset Rituals

- Meditation
- Audio
- Read

IDEAS

GOALS

Daily Log

BEST THINGS THAT HAPPENED TODAY

Date ___/___/___

Affirmations

Water 🍶🍶🍶🍶🍶

TODAY I AM GRATEFUL FOR

Mindset Rituals

- Meditation
- Audio
- Read

IDEAS	GOALS

Daily Log

BEST THINGS THAT HAPPENED TODAY

Date __/__/__

Affirmations

Water 🍼🍼🍼🍼🍼

TODAY I AM GRATEFUL FOR

Mindset Rituals

- Meditation
- Audio
- Read

IDEAS	GOALS

Daily Log

BEST THINGS THAT HAPPENED TODAY

Date __/__/__

Affirmations

Water 🍶🍶🍶🍶🍶

TODAY I AM GRATEFUL FOR

Mindset Rituals

- Meditation
- Audio
- Read

IDEAS	GOALS

Daily Log

BEST THINGS THAT HAPPENED TODAY

Date __/__/__

Affirmations

Water 🍾🍾🍾🍾🍾

TODAY I AM GRATEFUL FOR

Mindset Rituals

- Meditation
- Audio
- Read

IDEAS	GOALS

Daily Log

BEST THINGS THAT HAPPENED TODAY

Date ___/___/___

Affirmations

Water 🍼🍼🍼🍼🍼

TODAY I AM GRATEFUL FOR

Mindset Rituals

o   Meditation

o   Audio

o   Read

IDEAS	GOALS

Daily Log

BEST THINGS THAT HAPPENED TODAY

Date __/__/__

Affirmations

Water 🍶🍶🍶🍶🍶

TODAY I AM GRATEFUL FOR

Mindset Rituals

o Meditation

o Audio

o Read

IDEAS | GOALS

Daily Log

BEST THINGS THAT HAPPENED TODAY

Date __/__/__

Affirmations

Water 🍶🍶🍶🍶🍶

TODAY I AM GRATEFUL FOR

Mindset Rituals

- Meditation
- Audio
- Read

IDEAS	GOALS

Daily Log

BEST THINGS THAT HAPPENED TODAY

Date __/__/__

Affirmations

Water 🍼🍼🍼🍼🍼

TODAY I AM GRATEFUL FOR

Mindset Rituals

- Meditation
- Audio
- Read

IDEAS	GOALS

Daily Log

BEST THINGS THAT HAPPENED TODAY

Date ___/___/___

Affirmations

Water 🍼🍼🍼🍼🍼

TODAY I AM GRATEFUL FOR

Mindset Rituals

- Meditation
- Audio
- Read

IDEAS	GOALS

Daily Log

BEST THINGS THAT HAPPENED TODAY

Date __/__/__

Affirmations

Water 🍶🍶🍶🍶🍶

TODAY I AM GRATEFUL FOR

Mindset Rituals

- Meditation
- Audio
- Read

IDEAS	GOALS

Daily Log

BEST THINGS THAT HAPPENED TODAY

Date ___/___/___

Water 🍼🍼🍼🍼

Affirmations

TODAY I AM GRATEFUL FOR

Mindset Rituals

- Meditation
- Audio
- Read

IDEAS	GOALS

Daily Log

BEST THINGS THAT HAPPENED TODAY

Date __/__/__

Affirmations

Water 🍼🍼🍼🍼🍼

TODAY I AM GRATEFUL FOR

Mindset Rituals

- ○ Meditation
- ○ Audio
- ○ Read

IDEAS	GOALS

Daily Log

BEST THINGS THAT HAPPENED TODAY

Date __/__/__

Affirmations

Water

TODAY I AM GRATEFUL FOR

Mindset Rituals

o Meditation

o Audio

o Read

IDEAS

GOALS

Daily Log

BEST THINGS THAT HAPPENED TODAY

Date __/__/__

Affirmations

Water 🍼🍼🍼🍼🍼

TODAY I AM GRATEFUL FOR

Mindset Rituals

- Meditation
- Audio
- Read

IDEAS

GOALS

Daily Log

BEST THINGS THAT HAPPENED TODAY

Date ___/___/___

Affirmations

Water 🍼🍼🍼🍼🍼

TODAY I AM GRATEFUL FOR

Mindset Rituals

- Meditation
- Audio
- Read

IDEAS	GOALS

Daily Log

BEST THINGS THAT HAPPENED TODAY

Date __/__/__

Affirmations

Water

TODAY I AM GRATEFUL FOR

Mindset Rituals

- Meditation
- Audio
- Read

IDEAS	GOALS

Daily Log

BEST THINGS THAT HAPPENED TODAY

Date ___/___/___

Affirmations

Water 🍶🍶🍶🍶🍶

TODAY I AM GRATEFUL FOR

Mindset Rituals

- Meditation
- Audio
- Read

IDEAS	GOALS

Daily Log

BEST THINGS THAT HAPPENED TODAY

Date __/__/__

Affirmations

Water

TODAY I AM GRATEFUL FOR

Mindset Rituals

- Meditation
- Audio
- Read

IDEAS

GOALS

Daily Log

BEST THINGS THAT HAPPENED TODAY

Date __/__/__

Affirmations

Water 🍶🍶🍶🍶🍶

TODAY I AM GRATEFUL FOR

Mindset Rituals

- Meditation
- Audio
- Read

IDEAS	GOALS

Daily Log

BEST THINGS THAT HAPPENED TODAY

Date __/__/__

Affirmations

Water 🍶🍶🍶🍶🍶

TODAY I AM GRATEFUL FOR

Mindset Rituals

- Meditation
- Audio
- Read

IDEAS	GOALS

Daily Log

BEST THINGS THAT HAPPENED TODAY

*Date*___/___/___

Affirmations

Water 🍼🍼🍼🍼🍼

TODAY I AM GRATEFUL FOR

Mindset Rituals

- Meditation
- Audio
- Read

IDEAS	GOALS

Daily Log

BEST THINGS THAT HAPPENED TODAY

Date ___/___/___

Affirmations

Water 🍶🍶🍶🍶🍶

TODAY I AM GRATEFUL FOR

Mindset Rituals

- Meditation
- Audio
- Read

IDEAS

GOALS

Daily Log

BEST THINGS THAT HAPPENED TODAY

Date __/__/__

Affirmations

Water 🍶🍶🍶🍶🍶

TODAY I AM GRATEFUL FOR

Mindset Rituals

- Meditation
- Audio
- Read

IDEAS

GOALS

Daily Log

BEST THINGS THAT HAPPENED TODAY

Date __/__/__

Affirmations

Water 🍼🍼🍼🍼🍼

TODAY I AM GRATEFUL FOR

Mindset Rituals

- Meditation
- Audio
- Read

IDEAS	GOALS

Daily Log

BEST THINGS THAT HAPPENED TODAY

Date ___/___/___

Affirmations

Water 🍶🍶🍶🍶🍶

TODAY I AM GRATEFUL FOR

Mindset Rituals

- Meditation
- Audio
- Read

IDEAS	GOALS

Daily Log

BEST THINGS THAT HAPPENED TODAY

Date __/__/__

Affirmations

Water 🍍🍍🍍🍍🍍

TODAY I AM GRATEFUL FOR

Mindset Rituals

- Meditation
- Audio
- Read

IDEAS	GOALS

Daily Log

BEST THINGS THAT HAPPENED TODAY

Date ___/___/___

Affirmations

Water 🍶🍶🍶🍶🍶

TODAY I AM GRATEFUL FOR

Mindset Rituals

- Meditation
- Audio
- Read

IDEAS	GOALS

Daily Log

BEST THINGS THAT HAPPENED TODAY

Date __/__/__

Affirmations

Water 🍶🍶🍶🍶🍶

TODAY I AM GRATEFUL FOR

Mindset Rituals

- Meditation
- Audio
- Read

IDEAS	GOALS

Daily Log

BEST THINGS THAT HAPPENED TODAY

Date __/__/__

Affirmations

Water 🍶🍶🍶🍶🍶

TODAY I AM GRATEFUL FOR

Mindset Rituals

o Meditation

o Audio

o Read

IDEAS

GOALS

Daily Log

BEST THINGS THAT HAPPENED TODAY

Date __/__/__

Affirmations

Water 🍶🍶🍶🍶🍶

TODAY I AM GRATEFUL FOR

Mindset Rituals

- Meditation
- Audio
- Read

IDEAS

GOALS

Daily Log

BEST THINGS THAT HAPPENED TODAY

Date ___/___/___

Affirmations

Water 🍼🍼🍼🍼🍼

TODAY I AM GRATEFUL FOR

Mindset Rituals

- Meditation
- Audio
- Read

IDEAS	GOALS

Daily Log

BEST THINGS THAT HAPPENED TODAY

Date ___/___/___

Affirmations

Water 🍼🍼🍼🍼🍼

TODAY I AM GRATEFUL FOR

Mindset Rituals

- Meditation
- Audio
- Read

IDEAS	GOALS

Daily Log

BEST THINGS THAT HAPPENED TODAY

Date ___/___/___

Affirmations

Water 🍍🍍🍍🍍🍍

TODAY I AM GRATEFUL FOR

Mindset Rituals

- Meditation
- Audio
- Read

IDEAS	GOALS

Daily Log

BEST THINGS THAT HAPPENED TODAY

Date ___/___/___

Affirmations

Water 🍼🍼🍼🍼🍼

TODAY I AM GRATEFUL FOR

Mindset Rituals

- Meditation
- Audio
- Read

IDEAS

GOALS

Daily Log

BEST THINGS THAT HAPPENED TODAY

Date ___/___/___

Affirmations

Water 🍼🍼🍼🍼🍼

TODAY I AM GRATEFUL FOR

Mindset Rituals

- Meditation
- Audio
- Read

IDEAS	GOALS

Daily Log

BEST THINGS THAT HAPPENED TODAY

Date __/__/__

Affirmations

Water 🍶🍶🍶🍶🍶

TODAY I AM GRATEFUL FOR

Mindset Rituals

- Meditation
- Audio
- Read

IDEAS	GOALS

Daily Log

BEST THINGS THAT HAPPENED TODAY

Date ___/___/___

Affirmations

Water 🍼🍼🍼🍼🍼

TODAY I AM GRATEFUL FOR

Mindset Rituals

- Meditation
- Audio
- Read

IDEAS	GOALS

Daily Log

BEST THINGS THAT HAPPENED TODAY

Date ___/___/___

Affirmations

Water 🍼🍼🍼🍼🍼

TODAY I AM GRATEFUL FOR

Mindset Rituals

- Meditation
- Audio
- Read

IDEAS

GOALS

Daily Log

BEST THINGS THAT HAPPENED TODAY

Date __/__/__

Affirmations

Water 🍶🍶🍶🍶🍶

TODAY I AM GRATEFUL FOR

Mindset Rituals

- Meditation
- Audio
- Read

IDEAS	GOALS

Daily Log

BEST THINGS THAT HAPPENED TODAY

Date __/__/__

Affirmations

Water

TODAY I AM GRATEFUL FOR

Mindset Rituals

- Meditation
- Audio
- Read

IDEAS	GOALS

Daily Log

BEST THINGS THAT HAPPENED TODAY

Date __/__/__

Affirmations

Water 🍼🍼🍼🍼

TODAY I AM GRATEFUL FOR

Mindset Rituals

- Meditation
- Audio
- Read

IDEAS	GOALS

Daily Log

BEST THINGS THAT HAPPENED TODAY

Date ___/___/___

Affirmations

Water 🍶🍶🍶🍶🍶

TODAY I AM GRATEFUL FOR

Mindset Rituals

- Meditation
- Audio
- Read

IDEAS

GOALS

Daily Log

BEST THINGS THAT HAPPENED TODAY

Date ___/___/___

Affirmations

Water 🍼🍼🍼🍼

TODAY I AM GRATEFUL FOR

Mindset Rituals

- Meditation
- Audio
- Read

IDEAS	GOALS

Daily Log

BEST THINGS THAT HAPPENED TODAY

Date __/__/__

Affirmations

Water 🍼🍼🍼🍼🍼

TODAY I AM GRATEFUL FOR

Mindset Rituals

- Meditation
- Audio
- Read

IDEAS	GOALS

Daily Log

BEST THINGS THAT HAPPENED TODAY

Date __/__/__

Affirmations

Water 🍼🍼🍼🍼

TODAY I AM GRATEFUL FOR

Mindset Rituals

- Meditation
- Audio
- Read

IDEAS	GOALS

Daily Log

BEST THINGS THAT HAPPENED TODAY

Date ___/___/___

Affirmations

Water 🍶🍶🍶🍶🍶

TODAY I AM GRATEFUL FOR

Mindset Rituals

- Meditation
- Audio
- Read

IDEAS

GOALS

Daily Log

BEST THINGS THAT HAPPENED TODAY

Date __/__/__

Affirmations

Water 🍶🍶🍶🍶🍶

TODAY I AM GRATEFUL FOR

Mindset Rituals

- Meditation
- Audio
- Read

IDEAS	GOALS

Daily Log

BEST THINGS THAT HAPPENED TODAY

Date __/__/__

Affirmations

Water 🍶🍶🍶🍶🍶

TODAY I AM GRATEFUL FOR

Mindset Rituals

- Meditation
- Audio
- Read

IDEAS

GOALS

Daily Log

BEST THINGS THAT HAPPENED TODAY

Date __/__/__

Affirmations

Water 🍼🍼🍼🍼🍼

TODAY I AM GRATEFUL FOR

Mindset Rituals

- Meditation
- Audio
- Read

IDEAS	GOALS

Daily Log

BEST THINGS THAT HAPPENED TODAY

Date __/__/__

Affirmations

Water 🍼🍼🍼🍼🍼

TODAY I AM GRATEFUL FOR

Mindset Rituals

- Meditation
- Audio
- Read

IDEAS

GOALS

Daily Log

BEST THINGS THAT HAPPENED TODAY

Date __/__/__

Affirmations

Water 🍼🍼🍼🍼🍼

TODAY I AM GRATEFUL FOR

Mindset Rituals

- Meditation
- Audio
- Read

IDEAS	GOALS

Daily Log

BEST THINGS THAT HAPPENED TODAY

Date __/__/__

Water 🍶🍶🍶🍶🍶

Affirmations

TODAY I AM GRATEFUL FOR

Mindset Rituals

o Meditation

o Audio

o Read

IDEAS	GOALS

Daily Log

BEST THINGS THAT HAPPENED TODAY

Date ___/___/___

Affirmations

Water 🍼🍼🍼🍼🍼

TODAY I AM GRATEFUL FOR

Mindset Rituals

- Meditation
- Audio
- Read

IDEAS	GOALS

Daily Log

BEST THINGS THAT HAPPENED TODAY

Date __/__/__

Water 🍶🍶🍶🍶🍶

Affirmations

TODAY I AM GRATEFUL FOR

Mindset Rituals

- Meditation
- Audio
- Read

IDEAS	GOALS

Daily Log

BEST THINGS THAT HAPPENED TODAY

Date ___/___/___

Affirmations

Water 🍼🍼🍼🍼🍼

TODAY I AM GRATEFUL FOR

Mindset Rituals

- Meditation
- Audio
- Read

IDEAS	GOALS

Daily Log

BEST THINGS THAT HAPPENED TODAY

Date __/__/__

Affirmations

Water 🍍🍍🍍🍍🍍

TODAY I AM GRATEFUL FOR

Mindset Rituals

- Meditation
- Audio
- Read

IDEAS	GOALS

Daily Log

BEST THINGS THAT HAPPENED TODAY

Date ___/___/___

Affirmations

Water 🍶🍶🍶🍶🍶

TODAY I AM GRATEFUL FOR

Mindset Rituals

- Meditation
- Audio
- Read

IDEAS	GOALS

Daily Log

BEST THINGS THAT HAPPENED TODAY

Date ___/___/___

Affirmations

Water 🍼🍼🍼🍼🍼

TODAY I AM GRATEFUL FOR

Mindset Rituals

- Meditation
- Audio
- Read

IDEAS	GOALS

Daily Log

BEST THINGS THAT HAPPENED TODAY

Date __/__/__

Affirmations

Water 🍶🍶🍶🍶🍶

TODAY I AM GRATEFUL FOR

Mindset Rituals

o Meditation

o Audio

o Read

IDEAS	GOALS

Daily Log

BEST THINGS THAT HAPPENED TODAY

Date __/__/__

Affirmations

Water 🍶🍶🍶🍶🍶

TODAY I AM GRATEFUL FOR

Mindset Rituals

- Meditation
- Audio
- Read

IDEAS

GOALS

Daily Log

BEST THINGS THAT HAPPENED TODAY

Date __/__/__

Affirmations

Water 🍼🍼🍼🍼

TODAY I AM GRATEFUL FOR

Mindset Rituals

- Meditation
- Audio
- Read

IDEAS

GOALS

Daily Log

BEST THINGS THAT HAPPENED TODAY

Date ___/___/___

Affirmations

Water 🍼🍼🍼🍼🍼

TODAY I AM GRATEFUL FOR

Mindset Rituals

- Meditation
- Audio
- Read

IDEAS

GOALS

Daily Log

BEST THINGS THAT HAPPENED TODAY

Date __/__/__

Affirmations

Water 🍼🍼🍼🍼🍼

TODAY I AM GRATEFUL FOR

Mindset Rituals

- Meditation
- Audio
- Read

IDEAS	GOALS

Daily Log

BEST THINGS THAT HAPPENED TODAY

Date ___/___/___

Affirmations

Water 🍼🍼🍼🍼🍼

TODAY I AM GRATEFUL FOR

Mindset Rituals

- Meditation
- Audio
- Read

IDEAS	GOALS

Daily Log

BEST THINGS THAT HAPPENED TODAY

Date __/__/__

Affirmations

Water

TODAY I AM GRATEFUL FOR

Mindset Rituals

- Meditation
- Audio
- Read

IDEAS	GOALS

Daily Log

BEST THINGS THAT HAPPENED TODAY

Date __/__/__

Water

Affirmations

TODAY I AM GRATEFUL FOR

Mindset Rituals

- Meditation
- Audio
- Read

IDEAS

GOALS

Daily Log

BEST THINGS THAT HAPPENED TODAY

Date ___/___/___

Affirmations

Water 🍶🍶🍶🍶🍶

TODAY I AM GRATEFUL FOR

Mindset Rituals

- Meditation
- Audio
- Read

IDEAS

GOALS

Daily Log

BEST THINGS THAT HAPPENED TODAY

Date ___/___/___

Affirmations

Water 🍼🍼🍼🍼🍼

TODAY I AM GRATEFUL FOR

Mindset Rituals

- Meditation
- Audio
- Read

IDEAS	GOALS

Daily Log

BEST THINGS THAT HAPPENED TODAY

Date __/__/__

Affirmations

Water 🍼🍼🍼🍼🍼

TODAY I AM GRATEFUL FOR

Mindset Rituals

- Meditation
- Audio
- Read

IDEAS	GOALS

Daily Log

BEST THINGS THAT HAPPENED TODAY

Date __/__/__

Affirmations

Water 🍼🍼🍼🍼🍼

TODAY I AM GRATEFUL FOR

Mindset Rituals

- ○ Meditation
- ○ Audio
- ○ Read

IDEAS

GOALS

Daily Log

BEST THINGS THAT HAPPENED TODAY

Date __/__/__

Affirmations

Water 🍶🍶🍶🍶🍶

TODAY I AM GRATEFUL FOR

Mindset Rituals

- Meditation
- Audio
- Read

IDEAS	GOALS

Daily Log

BEST THINGS THAT HAPPENED TODAY

Date __/__/__

Affirmations

Water 🍼🍼🍼🍼🍼

TODAY I AM GRATEFUL FOR

Mindset Rituals

- Meditation
- Audio
- Read

IDEAS

GOALS

Daily Log

BEST THINGS THAT HAPPENED TODAY

Date __/__/__

Affirmations

Water 🍶🍶🍶🍶🍶

TODAY I AM GRATEFUL FOR

Mindset Rituals

- Meditation
- Audio
- Read

IDEAS

GOALS

Daily Log

BEST THINGS THAT HAPPENED TODAY

Date __/__/__

Water 🍶🍶🍶🍶🍶

Affirmations

TODAY I AM GRATEFUL FOR

Mindset Rituals

- ○ Meditation
- ○ Audio
- ○ Read

IDEAS	GOALS

Daily Log

BEST THINGS THAT HAPPENED TODAY

Date __/__/__

Affirmations

Water 🍼🍼🍼🍼🍼

TODAY I AM GRATEFUL FOR

Mindset Rituals

- Meditation
- Audio
- Read

IDEAS	GOALS

Daily Log

BEST THINGS THAT HAPPENED TODAY

Date __/__/__

Water

Affirmations

TODAY I AM GRATEFUL FOR

Mindset Rituals

- Meditation
- Audio
- Read

IDEAS	GOALS

Daily Log

BEST THINGS THAT HAPPENED TODAY

Date __/__/__

Affirmations

Water 🍶🍶🍶🍶🍶

TODAY I AM GRATEFUL FOR

Mindset Rituals

- Meditation
- Audio
- Read

IDEAS	GOALS

Daily Log

BEST THINGS THAT HAPPENED TODAY

Date __/__/__

Affirmations

Water 🍶🍶🍶🍶🍶

TODAY I AM GRATEFUL FOR

Mindset Rituals

- Meditation
- Audio
- Read

IDEAS

GOALS

Daily Log

BEST THINGS THAT HAPPENED TODAY

Date __/__/__

Affirmations

Water 🍼🍼🍼🍼

TODAY I AM GRATEFUL FOR

Mindset Rituals

- Meditation
- Audio
- Read

IDEAS	GOALS

Daily Log

BEST THINGS THAT HAPPENED TODAY

Date __/__/__

Affirmations

Water

TODAY I AM GRATEFUL FOR

Mindset Rituals

- ○ Meditation
- ○ Audio
- ○ Read

IDEAS

GOALS

Daily Log

BEST THINGS THAT HAPPENED TODAY

Date __/__/__

Affirmations

Water 🍼🍼🍼🍼🍼

TODAY I AM GRATEFUL FOR

Mindset Rituals

- Meditation
- Audio
- Read

IDEAS	GOALS

Daily Log

BEST THINGS THAT HAPPENED TODAY

Date __/__/__

Affirmations

Water 🍶🍶🍶🍶🍶

TODAY I AM GRATEFUL FOR

Mindset Rituals

- Meditation
- Audio
- Read

IDEAS	GOALS

Daily Log

BEST THINGS THAT HAPPENED TODAY

Date __/__/__

Affirmations

Water 🍶🍶🍶🍶🍶

TODAY I AM GRATEFUL FOR

Mindset Rituals

- Meditation
- Audio
- Read

IDEAS	GOALS

Daily Log

BEST THINGS THAT HAPPENED TODAY

Date __/__/__

Affirmations

Water 🍼🍼🍼🍼🍼

TODAY I AM GRATEFUL FOR

Mindset Rituals

- Meditation
- Audio
- Read

IDEAS

GOALS

Daily Log

BEST THINGS THAT HAPPENED TODAY

Date __/__/__

Affirmations

Water 🍶🍶🍶🍶🍶

TODAY I AM GRATEFUL FOR

Mindset Rituals

o Meditation

o Audio

o Read

IDEAS

GOALS

Daily Log

BEST THINGS THAT HAPPENED TODAY

Date __/__/__

Affirmations

Water 🍶🍶🍶🍶🍶

TODAY I AM GRATEFUL FOR

Mindset Rituals

- Meditation
- Audio
- Read

IDEAS	GOALS

Daily Log

BEST THINGS THAT HAPPENED TODAY

Date __/__/__

Affirmations

Water 🍼🍼🍼🍼🍼

TODAY I AM GRATEFUL FOR

Mindset Rituals

- Meditation
- Audio
- Read

IDEAS	GOALS

Daily Log

BEST THINGS THAT HAPPENED TODAY

Date ___/___/___

Affirmations

Water 🍶🍶🍶🍶🍶

TODAY I AM GRATEFUL FOR

Mindset Rituals

- Meditation
- Audio
- Read

IDEAS

GOALS

Daily Log

BEST THINGS THAT HAPPENED TODAY

Date __/__/__

Affirmations

Water 🍶🍶🍶🍶🍶

TODAY I AM GRATEFUL FOR

Mindset Rituals

- Meditation
- Audio
- Read

IDEAS

GOALS

Daily Log

BEST THINGS THAT HAPPENED TODAY

Date __/__/__

Affirmations

Water

TODAY I AM GRATEFUL FOR

Mindset Rituals

- Meditation
- Audio
- Read

IDEAS

GOALS

Daily Log

BEST THINGS THAT HAPPENED TODAY

Date ___/___/___

Water 🍼🍼🍼🍼🍼

Affirmations

TODAY I AM GRATEFUL FOR

Mindset Rituals

- Meditation
- Audio
- Read

IDEAS	GOALS

Daily Log

BEST THINGS THAT HAPPENED TODAY

Date ___/___/___

Affirmations

Water 🍼🍼🍼🍼🍼

TODAY I AM GRATEFUL FOR

Mindset Rituals

- Meditation
- Audio
- Read

IDEAS

GOALS

Daily Log

BEST THINGS THAT HAPPENED TODAY

Date ___/___/___

Affirmations

Water 🍶🍶🍶🍶🍶

TODAY I AM GRATEFUL FOR

Mindset Rituals

- Meditation
- Audio
- Read

IDEAS	GOALS

Daily Log

BEST THINGS THAT HAPPENED TODAY

Date __/__/__

Water

Affirmations

TODAY I AM GRATEFUL FOR

Mindset Rituals

- Meditation
- Audio
- Read

IDEAS	GOALS

Daily Log

BEST THINGS THAT HAPPENED TODAY

Date ___/___/___

Affirmations

Water

TODAY I AM GRATEFUL FOR

Mindset Rituals

- Meditation
- Audio
- Read

IDEAS	GOALS

Daily Log

BEST THINGS THAT HAPPENED TODAY

Date ___/___/___

Affirmations

Water 🍶🍶🍶🍶🍶

TODAY I AM GRATEFUL FOR

Mindset Rituals

- Meditation
- Audio
- Read

IDEAS	GOALS

Daily Log

BEST THINGS THAT HAPPENED TODAY

Date __/__/__

Water 🍼🍼🍼🍼🍼

Affirmations

TODAY I AM GRATEFUL FOR

Mindset Rituals

- Meditation
- Audio
- Read

IDEAS	GOALS

Daily Log

BEST THINGS THAT HAPPENED TODAY

NWMC Masterclass

Date ___/___/___

Affirmations

Water 🍍🍍🍍🍍🍍

TODAY I AM GRATEFUL FOR

Mindset Rituals

- Meditation
- Audio
- Read

IDEAS	GOALS

Daily Log

BEST THINGS THAT HAPPENED TODAY

Date __/__/__

Affirmations

Water 🥤🥤🥤🥤🥤

TODAY I AM GRATEFUL FOR

Mindset Rituals

- Meditation
- Audio
- Read

IDEAS	GOALS

Daily Log

BEST THINGS THAT HAPPENED TODAY

Date ___/___/___

Affirmations

Water 🍶🍶🍶🍶🍶

TODAY I AM GRATEFUL FOR

Mindset Rituals

- Meditation
- Audio
- Read

IDEAS	GOALS

Daily Log

BEST THINGS THAT HAPPENED TODAY

NWMC Masterclass

Date __/__/__

Affirmations

Water 🍶🍶🍶🍶🍶

TODAY I AM GRATEFUL FOR

Mindset Rituals

- Meditation
- Audio
- Read

IDEAS	GOALS

Daily Log

BEST THINGS THAT HAPPENED TODAY

Date __/__/__

Affirmations

Water 🍶🍶🍶🍶🍶

TODAY I AM GRATEFUL FOR

Mindset Rituals

- Meditation
- Audio
- Read

IDEAS	GOALS

Daily Log

BEST THINGS THAT HAPPENED TODAY

Date __/__/__

Affirmations

Water 🍼🍼🍼🍼🍼

TODAY I AM GRATEFUL FOR

Mindset Rituals

- Meditation
- Audio
- Read

IDEAS	GOALS

Daily Log

BEST THINGS THAT HAPPENED TODAY

Date __/__/__

Affirmations

Water 🍶🍶🍶🍶🍶

TODAY I AM GRATEFUL FOR

Mindset Rituals

- Meditation
- Audio
- Read

IDEAS	GOALS

Daily Joy

BEST THINGS THAT HAPPENED TODAY

Date ___/___/___

Affirmations

Water 🍼🍼🍼🍼🍼

TODAY I AM GRATEFUL FOR

Mindset Rituals

- Meditation
- Audio
- Read

IDEAS	GOALS

Daily Log

BEST THINGS THAT HAPPENED TODAY

Date __/__/__

Affirmations

Water 🍼🍼🍼🍼🍼

TODAY I AM GRATEFUL FOR

Mindset Rituals

- Meditation
- Audio
- Read

IDEAS	GOALS

Daily Log

BEST THINGS THAT HAPPENED TODAY

Date __/__/__

Affirmations

Water 🍶🍶🍶🍶🍶

TODAY I AM GRATEFUL FOR

Mindset Rituals

- Meditation
- Audio
- Read

IDEAS	GOALS

Daily Log

BEST THINGS THAT HAPPENED TODAY

Date __/__/__

Affirmations

Water

TODAY I AM GRATEFUL FOR

Mindset Rituals

- Meditation
- Audio
- Read

IDEAS	GOALS

Daily Log

BEST THINGS THAT HAPPENED TODAY

Date __/__/__

Affirmations

Water 🍼🍼🍼🍼🍼

TODAY I AM GRATEFUL FOR

Mindset Rituals

- Meditation
- Audio
- Read

IDEAS	GOALS

Daily Log

BEST THINGS THAT HAPPENED TODAY

Date ___/___/___

Affirmations

Water 🍼🍼🍼🍼🍼

TODAY I AM GRATEFUL FOR

Mindset Rituals

- Meditation
- Audio
- Read

IDEAS

GOALS

Daily Log

BEST THINGS THAT HAPPENED TODAY

Date __/__/__

Affirmations

Water 🍶🍶🍶🍶🍶

TODAY I AM GRATEFUL FOR

Mindset Rituals

- Meditation
- Audio
- Read

IDEAS	GOALS

Daily Log

BEST THINGS THAT HAPPENED TODAY

Date ___/___/___

Affirmations

Water 🍶🍶🍶🍶🍶

TODAY I AM GRATEFUL FOR

Mindset Rituals

- Meditation
- Audio
- Read

IDEAS	GOALS

Daily Log

BEST THINGS THAT HAPPENED TODAY

Date __/__/__

Affirmations

Water 🍶🍶🍶🍶🍶

TODAY I AM GRATEFUL FOR

Mindset Rituals

- Meditation
- Audio
- Read

IDEAS	GOALS

Daily Log

BEST THINGS THAT HAPPENED TODAY

Date ___/___/___

Affirmations

Water 🍼🍼🍼🍼🍼

TODAY I AM GRATEFUL FOR

Mindset Rituals

- Meditation
- Audio
- Read

IDEAS	GOALS

Daily Log

BEST THINGS THAT HAPPENED TODAY

Date __/__/__

Affirmations

Water 🍶🍶🍶🍶🍶

TODAY I AM GRATEFUL FOR

Mindset Rituals

- Meditation
- Audio
- Read

IDEAS	GOALS

Daily Log

BEST THINGS THAT HAPPENED TODAY

Date ___/___/___

Affirmations

Water 🍶🍶🍶🍶🍶

TODAY I AM GRATEFUL FOR

Mindset Rituals

- Meditation
- Audio
- Read

IDEAS

GOALS

Daily Log

BEST THINGS THAT HAPPENED TODAY

Date ___/___/___

Affirmations

Water 🍼🍼🍼🍼🍼

TODAY I AM GRATEFUL FOR

Mindset Rituals

- Meditation
- Audio
- Read

IDEAS	GOALS

Daily Log

BEST THINGS THAT HAPPENED TODAY

Date ___/___/___

Affirmations

Water 🍶🍶🍶🍶🍶

TODAY I AM GRATEFUL FOR

Mindset Rituals

- Meditation
- Audio
- Read

IDEAS	GOALS

Daily Log

BEST THINGS THAT HAPPENED TODAY

Date___/___/___

Affirmations

Water 🍼🍼🍼🍼🍼

TODAY I AM GRATEFUL FOR

Mindset Rituals

- Meditation
- Audio
- Read

IDEAS	GOALS

Daily Log

BEST THINGS THAT HAPPENED TODAY

Date ___/___/___

Affirmations

Water 🍼🍼🍼🍼🍼

TODAY I AM GRATEFUL FOR

Mindset Rituals

- Meditation
- Audio
- Read

IDEAS

GOALS

Daily Log

BEST THINGS THAT HAPPENED TODAY

Date __/__/__

Affirmations

Water 🍍🍍🍍🍍🍍

TODAY I AM GRATEFUL FOR

Mindset Rituals

- Meditation
- Audio
- Read

IDEAS	GOALS

Daily Log

BEST THINGS THAT HAPPENED TODAY

Date __/__/__

Affirmations

Water 🍼🍼🍼🍼🍼

TODAY I AM GRATEFUL FOR

Mindset Rituals

- Meditation
- Audio
- Read

IDEAS	GOALS

Daily Log

BEST THINGS THAT HAPPENED TODAY

Date ___/___/___

Affirmations

Water 🍶🍶🍶🍶🍶

TODAY I AM GRATEFUL FOR

Mindset Rituals

- Meditation
- Audio
- Read

IDEAS	GOALS

Daily Log

BEST THINGS THAT HAPPENED TODAY

Date ___/___/___

Affirmations

Water 🍶🍶🍶🍶🍶

TODAY I AM GRATEFUL FOR

Mindset Rituals

- Meditation
- Audio
- Read

IDEAS	GOALS

Daily Log

BEST THINGS THAT HAPPENED TODAY

Date __/__/__

Affirmations

Water 🍼🍼🍼🍼🍼

TODAY I AM GRATEFUL FOR

Mindset Rituals

- Meditation
- Audio
- Read

IDEAS

GOALS

Daily Log

BEST THINGS THAT HAPPENED TODAY

Date ___/___/___

Affirmations

Water 🍼🍼🍼🍼🍼

TODAY I AM GRATEFUL FOR

Mindset Rituals

- Meditation
- Audio
- Read

IDEAS	GOALS

Daily Log

BEST THINGS THAT HAPPENED TODAY

Date __/__/__

Affirmations

Water 🍶🍶🍶🍶🍶

TODAY I AM GRATEFUL FOR

Mindset Rituals

- Meditation
- Audio
- Read

IDEAS	GOALS

Daily Log

BEST THINGS THAT HAPPENED TODAY

Date __/__/__

Affirmations

Water 🍶🍶🍶🍶🍶

TODAY I AM GRATEFUL FOR

Mindset Rituals

- Meditation
- Audio
- Read

IDEAS	GOALS

Daily Log

BEST THINGS THAT HAPPENED TODAY

Date __/__/__

Affirmations

Water 🍶🍶🍶🍶🍶

TODAY I AM GRATEFUL FOR

Mindset Rituals

- Meditation
- Audio
- Read

IDEAS	GOALS

Daily Log

BEST THINGS THAT HAPPENED TODAY

Date __/__/__

Affirmations

Water

TODAY I AM GRATEFUL FOR

Mindset Rituals

- Meditation
- Audio
- Read

IDEAS	GOALS

Daily Log

BEST THINGS THAT HAPPENED TODAY

Date ___/___/___

Affirmations

Water 🍼🍼🍼🍼🍼

TODAY I AM GRATEFUL FOR

Mindset Rituals

- Meditation
- Audio
- Read

IDEAS	GOALS

Daily Log

BEST THINGS THAT HAPPENED TODAY

Date __/__/__

Affirmations

Water 🍼🍼🍼🍼🍼

TODAY I AM GRATEFUL FOR

Mindset Rituals

- Meditation
- Audio
- Read

IDEAS	GOALS

Daily Log

BEST THINGS THAT HAPPENED TODAY

Date __/__/__

Affirmations

Water 🍼🍼🍼🍼🍼

TODAY I AM GRATEFUL FOR

Mindset Rituals

- Meditation
- Audio
- Read

IDEAS	GOALS

Daily Log

BEST THINGS THAT HAPPENED TODAY

Date ___/___/___

Affirmations

Water 🍶🍶🍶🍶🍶

TODAY I AM GRATEFUL FOR

Mindset Rituals

- Meditation
- Audio
- Read

IDEAS	GOALS

Daily Log

BEST THINGS THAT HAPPENED TODAY

Date ___/___/___

Affirmations

Water 🍶🍶🍶🍶🍶

TODAY I AM GRATEFUL FOR

Mindset Rituals

- Meditation
- Audio
- Read

IDEAS	GOALS

Daily Log

BEST THINGS THAT HAPPENED TODAY

Date ___/___/___

Affirmations

Water 🍼🍼🍼🍼🍼

TODAY I AM GRATEFUL FOR

Mindset Rituals

- Meditation
- Audio
- Read

IDEAS

GOALS

Daily Log

BEST THINGS THAT HAPPENED TODAY

Date __/__/__

Affirmations

Water 🍶🍶🍶🍶🍶

TODAY I AM GRATEFUL FOR

Mindset Rituals

- Meditation
- Audio
- Read

IDEAS	GOALS

Daily Log

BEST THINGS THAT HAPPENED TODAY

Date ___/___/___

Affirmations

Water 🍼🍼🍼🍼🍼

TODAY I AM GRATEFUL FOR

Mindset Rituals

- Meditation
- Audio
- Read

IDEAS	GOALS

Daily Log

BEST THINGS THAT HAPPENED TODAY

Date __/__/__

Affirmations

Water 🍼🍼🍼🍼🍼

TODAY I AM GRATEFUL FOR

Mindset Rituals

- Meditation
- Audio
- Read

IDEAS	GOALS

Daily Log

BEST THINGS THAT HAPPENED TODAY

Date __/__/__

Affirmations

Water 🍶🍶🍶🍶🍶

TODAY I AM GRATEFUL FOR

Mindset Rituals

- ○ Meditation
- ○ Audio
- ○ Read

IDEAS	GOALS

Daily Log

BEST THINGS THAT HAPPENED TODAY

Date __/__/__

Affirmations

Water

TODAY I AM GRATEFUL FOR

Mindset Rituals

- Meditation
- Audio
- Read

IDEAS	GOALS

Daily Log

BEST THINGS THAT HAPPENED TODAY

Date __/__/__

Affirmations

Water 🍶🍶🍶🍶🍶

TODAY I AM GRATEFUL FOR

Mindset Rituals

- Meditation
- Audio
- Read

IDEAS	GOALS

Daily Log

BEST THINGS THAT HAPPENED TODAY

*Date*___/___/___

Affirmations

Water 🍶🍶🍶🍶🍶

TODAY I AM GRATEFUL FOR

Mindset Rituals

- Meditation
- Audio
- Read

IDEAS	GOALS

Daily Log

BEST THINGS THAT HAPPENED TODAY

Date __/__/__

Affirmations

Water 🍼🍼🍼🍼🍼

TODAY I AM GRATEFUL FOR

Mindset Rituals

o Meditation

o Audio

o Read

IDEAS	GOALS

Daily Log

BEST THINGS THAT HAPPENED TODAY

Date ___/___/___

Affirmations

Water 🍶🍶🍶🍶🍶

TODAY I AM GRATEFUL FOR

Mindset Rituals

- Meditation
- Audio
- Read

IDEAS	GOALS

Daily Log

BEST THINGS THAT HAPPENED TODAY

Date __/__/__

Affirmations

Water 🍶🍶🍶🍶🍶

TODAY I AM GRATEFUL FOR

Mindset Rituals

- Meditation
- Audio
- Read

IDEAS	GOALS

Daily Log

BEST THINGS THAT HAPPENED TODAY

Date __/__/__

Affirmations

Water

TODAY I AM GRATEFUL FOR

Mindset Rituals

- Meditation
- Audio
- Read

IDEAS	GOALS

Daily Log

BEST THINGS THAT HAPPENED TODAY

Date ___/___/___

Affirmations

Water 🍶🍶🍶🍶🍶

TODAY I AM GRATEFUL FOR

Mindset Rituals

- Meditation
- Audio
- Read

IDEAS	GOALS

Daily Log

BEST THINGS THAT HAPPENED TODAY

Date __/__/__

Affirmations

Water 🍼🍼🍼🍼🍼

TODAY I AM GRATEFUL FOR

Mindset Rituals

- Meditation
- Audio
- Read

IDEAS	GOALS

Daily Log

BEST THINGS THAT HAPPENED TODAY

Date __/__/__

Affirmations

Water 🍶🍶🍶🍶🍶

TODAY I AM GRATEFUL FOR

Mindset Rituals

- Meditation
- Audio
- Read

IDEAS	GOALS

Daily Log

BEST THINGS THAT HAPPENED TODAY

Date __/__/__

Affirmations

Water

TODAY I AM GRATEFUL FOR

Mindset Rituals

- Meditation
- Audio
- Read

IDEAS	GOALS

Daily Log

BEST THINGS THAT HAPPENED TODAY

Date __/__/__

Affirmations

Water 🍶🍶🍶🍶🍶

TODAY I AM GRATEFUL FOR

Mindset Rituals

- Meditation
- Audio
- Read

IDEAS	GOALS

Daily Log

BEST THINGS THAT HAPPENED TODAY

Date __/__/__

Affirmations

Water 🍼🍼🍼🍼🍼

TODAY I AM GRATEFUL FOR

Mindset Rituals

- Meditation
- Audio
- Read

IDEAS	GOALS

Daily Log

BEST THINGS THAT HAPPENED TODAY

Date ___/___/___

Affirmations

Water 🍶🍶🍶🍶🍶

TODAY I AM GRATEFUL FOR

Mindset Rituals

- Meditation
- Audio
- Read

IDEAS	GOALS

Daily Log

BEST THINGS THAT HAPPENED TODAY

Date __/__/__

Affirmations

Water 🍶🍶🍶🍶🍶

TODAY I AM GRATEFUL FOR

Mindset Rituals

- Meditation
- Audio
- Read

IDEAS	GOALS

Daily Log

BEST THINGS THAT HAPPENED TODAY

Date __/__/__

Affirmations

Water 🍶🍶🍶🍶🍶

TODAY I AM GRATEFUL FOR

Mindset Rituals

- Meditation
- Audio
- Read

IDEAS	GOALS

Daily Log

BEST THINGS THAT HAPPENED TODAY

Date __/__/__

Affirmations

Water 🍶🍶🍶🍶🍶

TODAY I AM GRATEFUL FOR

Mindset Rituals

- Meditation
- Audio
- Read

IDEAS	GOALS

Daily Log

BEST THINGS THAT HAPPENED TODAY

Date __/__/__

Affirmations

Water 🍶🍶🍶🍶🍶

TODAY I AM GRATEFUL FOR

Mindset Rituals

- Meditation
- Audio
- Read

IDEAS	GOALS

Daily Log

BEST THINGS THAT HAPPENED TODAY

Date __/__/__

Affirmations

Water

TODAY I AM GRATEFUL FOR

Mindset Rituals

- Meditation
- Audio
- Read

IDEAS	GOALS

Daily Log

BEST THINGS THAT HAPPENED TODAY

Date __/__/__

Affirmations

Water

TODAY I AM GRATEFUL FOR

Mindset Rituals

- ○ Meditation
- ○ Audio
- ○ Read

IDEAS	GOALS

Daily Log

BEST THINGS THAT HAPPENED TODAY

Date ___/___/___

Affirmations

Water 🍼🍼🍼🍼🍼

TODAY I AM GRATEFUL FOR

Mindset Rituals

- Meditation
- Audio
- Read

IDEAS	GOALS

Daily Log

BEST THINGS THAT HAPPENED TODAY

Date ___/___/___

Affirmations

Water 🍶🍶🍶🍶🍶

TODAY I AM GRATEFUL FOR

Mindset Rituals

- Meditation
- Audio
- Read

IDEAS	GOALS

Daily Log

BEST THINGS THAT HAPPENED TODAY

NWMC Masterclass

Date __/__/__

Affirmations

Water

TODAY I AM GRATEFUL FOR

Mindset Rituals

- Meditation
- Audio
- Read

IDEAS	GOALS

Daily Log

BEST THINGS THAT HAPPENED TODAY

Date ___/___/___

Affirmations

Water 🍶🍶🍶🍶🍶

TODAY I AM GRATEFUL FOR

Mindset Rituals

- Meditation
- Audio
- Read

IDEAS	GOALS

Daily Log

BEST THINGS THAT HAPPENED TODAY

Date __/__/__

Affirmations

Water

TODAY I AM GRATEFUL FOR

Mindset Rituals

- Meditation
- Audio
- Read

IDEAS	GOALS

Daily Log

BEST THINGS THAT HAPPENED TODAY

Date ___/___/___

Affirmations

Water 🍶🍶🍶🍶🍶

TODAY I AM GRATEFUL FOR

Mindset Rituals

- Meditation
- Audio
- Read

IDEAS	GOALS

Daily Log

BEST THINGS THAT HAPPENED TODAY

Date ___/___/___

Affirmations

Water 🍼🍼🍼🍼🍼

TODAY I AM GRATEFUL FOR

Mindset Rituals

o Meditation

o Audio

o Read

IDEAS

GOALS

Daily Log

BEST THINGS THAT HAPPENED TODAY

Date ___/___/___

Affirmations

Water 🍶🍶🍶🍶🍶

TODAY I AM GRATEFUL FOR

Mindset Rituals

- Meditation
- Audio
- Read

IDEAS	GOALS

Daily Log

BEST THINGS THAT HAPPENED TODAY

Date __/__/__

Affirmations

Water 🍶🍶🍶🍶🍶

TODAY I AM GRATEFUL FOR

Mindset Rituals

- Meditation
- Audio
- Read

IDEAS	GOALS

Daily Log

BEST THINGS THAT HAPPENED TODAY

Date __/__/__

Affirmations

Water 🍶🍶🍶🍶🍶

TODAY I AM GRATEFUL FOR

Mindset Rituals

o Meditation

o Audio

o Read

IDEAS	GOALS

Daily Log

BEST THINGS THAT HAPPENED TODAY

Date ___/___/___

Affirmations

Water 🍼🍼🍼🍼🍼

TODAY I AM GRATEFUL FOR

Mindset Rituals

o Meditation

o Audio

o Read

IDEAS

GOALS

Daily Log

BEST THINGS THAT HAPPENED TODAY

Date __/__/__

Affirmations

Water

TODAY I AM GRATEFUL FOR

Mindset Rituals

- Meditation
- Audio
- Read

IDEAS	GOALS

Daily Log

BEST THINGS THAT HAPPENED TODAY

NWMC Masterclass

Date __/__/__

Affirmations

Water 🍼🍼🍼🍼🍼

TODAY I AM GRATEFUL FOR

Mindset Rituals

- Meditation
- Audio
- Read

IDEAS	GOALS

Daily Log

BEST THINGS THAT HAPPENED TODAY

Date ___/___/___

Affirmations

Water 🍶🍶🍶🍶🍶

TODAY I AM GRATEFUL FOR

Mindset Rituals

- Meditation
- Audio
- Read

IDEAS	GOALS

Daily Log

BEST THINGS THAT HAPPENED TODAY

Date __/__/__

Affirmations

Water

TODAY I AM GRATEFUL FOR

Mindset Rituals

- o Meditation
- o Audio
- o Read

IDEAS	GOALS

Daily Log

BEST THINGS THAT HAPPENED TODAY

Date ___/___/___

Affirmations

Water 🍶🍶🍶🍶🍶

TODAY I AM GRATEFUL FOR

Mindset Rituals

- ○ Meditation
- ○ Audio
- ○ Read

IDEAS	GOALS

Daily Log

BEST THINGS THAT HAPPENED TODAY

Date __/__/__

Affirmations

Water 🍼🍼🍼🍼🍼

TODAY I AM GRATEFUL FOR

Mindset Rituals

- Meditation
- Audio
- Read

IDEAS	GOALS

Daily Log

BEST THINGS THAT HAPPENED TODAY

Date __/__/__

Water 🍶🍶🍶🍶🍶

Affirmations

TODAY I AM GRATEFUL FOR

Mindset Rituals

- Meditation
- Audio
- Read

IDEAS	GOALS

Daily Log

BEST THINGS THAT HAPPENED TODAY

Date ___/___/___

Affirmations

Water 🍶🍶🍶🍶🍶

TODAY I AM GRATEFUL FOR

Mindset Rituals

- Meditation
- Audio
- Read

IDEAS	GOALS

Daily Log

BEST THINGS THAT HAPPENED TODAY

Date ___/___/___

Affirmations

Water 🍶🍶🍶🍶🍶

TODAY I AM GRATEFUL FOR

Mindset Rituals

- Meditation
- Audio
- Read

IDEAS

GOALS

Daily Log

BEST THINGS THAT HAPPENED TODAY

Date ___/___/___

Affirmations

Water 🍶🍶🍶🍶🍶

TODAY I AM GRATEFUL FOR

Mindset Rituals

- Meditation
- Audio
- Read

IDEAS | GOALS

Daily Log

BEST THINGS THAT HAPPENED TODAY

Date __/__/__

Affirmations

Water 🍼🍼🍼🍼🍼

TODAY I AM GRATEFUL FOR

Mindset Rituals

- Meditation
- Audio
- Read

IDEAS	GOALS

Daily Log

BEST THINGS THAT HAPPENED TODAY

Date ___/___/___

Affirmations

Water 🍼🍼🍼🍼🍼

TODAY I AM GRATEFUL FOR

Mindset Rituals

- Meditation
- Audio
- Read

IDEAS	GOALS

Daily Log

BEST THINGS THAT HAPPENED TODAY

Date ___/___/___

Affirmations

Water 🍍🍍🍍🍍🍍

TODAY I AM GRATEFUL FOR

Mindset Rituals

- Meditation
- Audio
- Read

IDEAS	GOALS

Daily Log

BEST THINGS THAT HAPPENED TODAY

Date __/__/__

Affirmations

Water 🍶🍶🍶🍶🍶

TODAY I AM GRATEFUL FOR

Mindset Rituals

- Meditation
- Audio
- Read

IDEAS	GOALS

Daily Log

BEST THINGS THAT HAPPENED TODAY

Date __/__/__

Affirmations

Water 🍼🍼🍼🍼

TODAY I AM GRATEFUL FOR

Mindset Rituals

- Meditation
- Audio
- Read

IDEAS	GOALS

Daily Log

BEST THINGS THAT HAPPENED TODAY

Date __/__/__

Affirmations

Water

TODAY I AM GRATEFUL FOR

Mindset Rituals

- Meditation
- Audio
- Read

IDEAS	GOALS

Daily Log

BEST THINGS THAT HAPPENED TODAY

Date __/__/__

Water

Affirmations

TODAY I AM GRATEFUL FOR

Mindset Rituals

- Meditation
- Audio
- Read

IDEAS	GOALS

Daily Log

BEST THINGS THAT HAPPENED TODAY

Date __/__/__

Affirmations

Water 🍶🍶🍶🍶🍶

TODAY I AM GRATEFUL FOR

Mindset Rituals

- Meditation
- Audio
- Read

IDEAS	GOALS

Daily Log

BEST THINGS THAT HAPPENED TODAY

Date __/__/__

Affirmations

Water 🍶🍶🍶🍶🍶

TODAY I AM GRATEFUL FOR

Mindset Rituals

- Meditation
- Audio
- Read

IDEAS	GOALS

Daily Log

BEST THINGS THAT HAPPENED TODAY

Date ___/___/___

Affirmations

Water 🍶🍶🍶🍶🍶

TODAY I AM GRATEFUL FOR

Mindset Rituals

- Meditation
- Audio
- Read

IDEAS	GOALS

Daily Log

BEST THINGS THAT HAPPENED TODAY

Date ___/___/___

Affirmations

Water 🍼🍼🍼🍼🍼

TODAY I AM GRATEFUL FOR

Mindset Rituals

- ○ Meditation
- ○ Audio
- ○ Read

IDEAS	GOALS

Daily Log

BEST THINGS THAT HAPPENED TODAY

Date ___/___/___

Affirmations

Water 🍼🍼🍼🍼🍼

TODAY I AM GRATEFUL FOR

Mindset Rituals

- Meditation
- Audio
- Read

IDEAS	GOALS

Daily Log

BEST THINGS THAT HAPPENED TODAY

Date ___/___/___

Affirmations

Water 🍼🍼🍼🍼🍼

TODAY I AM GRATEFUL FOR

Mindset Rituals

- Meditation
- Audio
- Read

IDEAS	GOALS

Daily Log

BEST THINGS THAT HAPPENED TODAY

Date __/__/__

Affirmations

Water 🍶🍶🍶🍶🍶

TODAY I AM GRATEFUL FOR

Mindset Rituals

- Meditation
- Audio
- Read

IDEAS	GOALS

Daily Log

BEST THINGS THAT HAPPENED TODAY

Resources

Ross Kumrou

Author - Podcaster - Coach & Mentor - Network Marketer

Check out more of my resources below to help you grow your network marketing business.
Feel free to reach out and give me a follow on Instagram @ross_kumrou

BOOK : NETWORK MARKETING MASTERCLASS
The Social Media Edition

Available now at amazon.co.uk. A fully interactive workbook full of golden nuggets & actual 'HOW TO'S' that can help anybody at any level in network marketing to help take their business to the next level.

ONLINE COURSE : 14 DAY MASTERCLASS

Spend 14 days with me personally as I take you through every aspect of Network Marketing and give you proven tips and strategies on recruitment, sales, how to connect with people, content, IGTV, Reels, FB Live, Leadership and much more including a 1-2-1 call and 12 month personal development plan. This an exclusive course limited to 20 spaces per month. Please email networkmarketingmasterclass@outlook.com for price and details.

FACEBOOK GROUP- THE TCC CLUB
The Consistency Club

Having been in network marketing for over 5 years I know the ONE thing that most people struggle with. Consistency. So I developed a daily action takers group where I go LIVE daily with set tasks & challenges to focus on each day to help keep you accountable to your business everyday without fail. I also host a goal setting session every month & give reward and recognition for the most consistent members in the club. Please email networkmarketingmasterclass@outlook.com for price and details.

PODCAST - NETWORK MARKETING MASTERCLASS

If you're anything like me then you'll know that listening to an audio everyday is an incredible tool to help grow your mindset, keep you focussed and absorb great value that you can implement straight away. If this is you then feel free to tune in to my training podcast for network marketers. Available on Apple podcasts, Spotify, Google & all major podcast hosts. Episodes air every Monday, Wednesday & Friday.

More online courses & books coming soon.

Printed in Great Britain
by Amazon